Just a Lucky So and So

The Story of Louis Armstrong

by Lesa Cline-Ransome
illustrated by James Ransome

Holiday House / New York

HOLIDAY HOUSE is registered in the U.S. Patent and Trademark Office
Printed and bound in October 2015 at Toppan Leefung, DongGuan City, China.
www.holidayhouse.com
First Edition
1 3 5 7 9 10 8 6 4 2

Library of Congress Cataloging-in-Publication Data
Cline-Ransome, Lesa, author.
Just a lucky so and so : the story of Louis Armstrong / by Lesa Cline-Ransome ; illustrated by James E. Ransome.
— First edition.
pages cm
ISBN 978-0-8234-3428-2 (hardcover)
1. Armstrong, Louis, 1901-1971—Juvenile literature. 2. Jazz musicians—United States—Biography—Juvenile literature.
I. Ransome, James, illustrator. II. Title.
ML3930.A75C55 2015
781.65092—dc23
[B]
2014038325

To Jean Cunningham and the late Robert M. Cunningham
Thanks for sharing your home, studio, love and lunches with me.
You are both my Joe Oliver!—*J. E. R.*

For my brother, William "Billy" Cline, Jr. whose love, support
and laughter made me one lucky so and so.—*L. C. R.*

In New Orleans, Louisiana, in a part of town outside of Storyville, tucked in a corner called Back o' Town, in a section nicknamed The Battlefield, Little Louis Armstrong was born, black and poor and lucky.

My whole life has been happiness.

On the corner of Perdido and Liberty, Little Louis lived in one room with no lights and no running water. But it was home to him and his sister, Mama Lucy, and his mama, Mayann.

The grandson of slaves, Little Louis toted laundry, hauled coal, sold newspapers and scavenged through garbage to earn money for his family. On the streets, Little Louis sometimes made his own trouble. But it was nothing his mama's sharp tongue and a switch from the chinaberry tree in Grandma Josephine's yard couldn't fix.

Every day, outside his window, Little Louis listened
up and down the streets, to the music of brass
bands, funeral marches, honky-tonks on Saturday
nights, church services on Sunday mornings.

Across the street, he peeked through the cracks of Funky Butt Hall. On cornet, the sassy ragtime music of Bunk Johnson, Buddy Bolden and Joe Oliver followed him wherever he went. Johnson had tone, Bolden blew hard. But for Little Louis, it was "King" Oliver who could outblow, outperform any horn player in all New Orleans.

The king of all musicians was Joe Oliver.

School learning at the Fisk School for Boys began for Little Louis at seven. Before school and after, on the Karnofskys' wagon, next to Morris, Little Louis tooted a tin horn. "Penny for your rags," and bleated, "Nickel for your scraps."

Although I could not play a good tune, Morris applauded me just the same.

Through the window of a pawnshop, a cornet caught Louis's eye. A five-dollar loan from Morris bought the cornet for Louis. Some brass polish and oil brought the horn to life.

Down Rampart Street, four boys harmonized "My Brazilian Beauty". Little Mack on drums, Big Nose Sidney on bass, Redhead Happy Bolton as baritone, and the gravelly tenor of Little Louis, the boy with a smile so wide open kids called him Satchelmouth.

New Year's Eve in New Orleans was all music, fireworks and midnight shots fired in celebration. Little Louis joined in with his stepfather's gun. All his scrapes with the law added up, and at eleven years, Little Louis was sent away.

I thought the world was coming to an end.

At the Colored Waif's Home for Boys, Little Louis could barely eat. He missed his mama, his sister, and his cornet. Through his open windows drifted the call of the bugle. A bugle to rise, a bugle for chores, a bugle for bed. The band leader, Mr. Davis told Little Louis that boys from The Battlefield don't belong in a band.

Little Louis sang solos for everyone to hear. Mr. Davis listened and started Louis with the tambourine. Then he played the drums. Mr. Davis made him the bugler, then he put him on cornet. Mr. Davis made him the bandleader.

Me and music got married at the home.

The band traveled to play in every corner of New Orleans: Uptown and Downtown, West End, Spanish Fort and Front o' Town. But for Little Louis, there was nothing like walking through his old neighborhood at the head of the band, blowing "Home Sweet Home." Lining the streets was everyone he knew, and right up front was his mama Mayann.

I could not think of anything but my good luck.

At fourteen, Little Louis returned to Perdido Street not so little. By then he could make any song swing. Louis needed to hear a song just once and it was his. He worked all day hauling coal and all night playing in honky-tonks around town.

Louis met Joe as Joe paraded through town with the Onward Brass Band and followed him everywhere. Louis ran Joe's errands, carried his horn. But in the between times, Joe taught Louis note by note. In Joe's home Louis filled up on rice and beans and music lessons. Louis traded in his first pawnshop cornet for Joe's used one.

I prized that horn and guarded it with my life.

Louis listened to Joe's horn crow like a rooster, growl like a lion, cry like a newborn baby. Two horns, side by side, so close, Louis called him Papa Joe. Aboard the SS Sidney, he blew swing, waltzes and dance tunes all up and down the banks of the Mississippi River. On land, Louis blew with the Tuxedo Brass Band and then Kid Ory's hottest jazz band in town, featuring Baby Dodds, Pops Foster and his Papa Joe Oliver.

When I pick up that horn, that's all. The world's behind me, and I don't concentrate on nothing but it. I love them notes.

After a time, New Orleans honky-tonks were too small for the King. Joe hopped a train and blew good-bye to New Orleans. Chicago was waiting. Louis stepped in where Joe stepped out. His horn had folks talking about the little boy from The Battlefield. Night after night, Louis filled up the halls, filled up the streets, filled up his pockets with the music from his cornet. Four years later, Joe sent a telegram. Louis was ready to leave.

He sent for me, and whatever he's doing I want to do it with him.

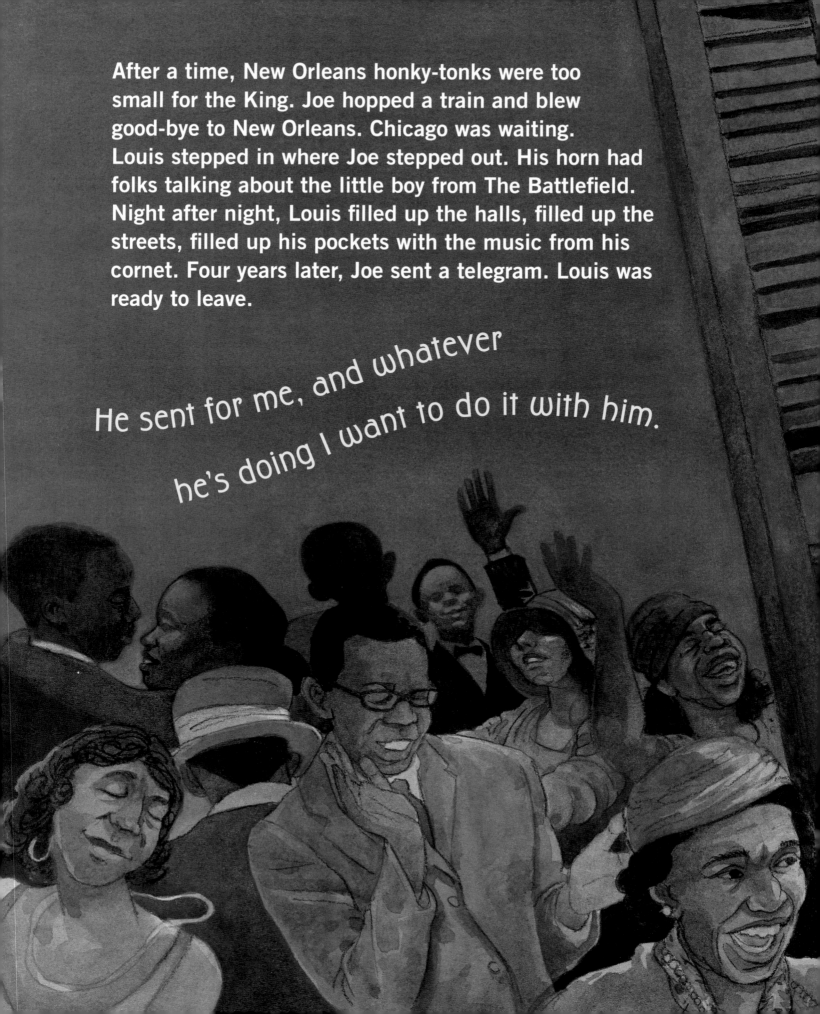

"All aboard!" Louis stood on the train platform, fish sandwich in one hand, cornet in the other. Worried he'd catch cold in the Windy City, his mama made him wear long johns in the August heat. Joe Oliver and Chicago were waiting.

I'd never seen a city that big.

On the South Side of Chicago, at the corner of Thirty-First and Cottage Grove, Louis peeked into Lincoln Gardens dance hall. A globe glittered from the ceiling. A balcony looked out over the dance floor. Joe and King Oliver's Creole Jazz Band warmed up.

Opening night always makes you feel as though little butterflies were running around in your stomach.

Louis's tuxedo was pressed and patched and small. He walked to the bandstand where Baby and Johnny Dodds, Lil Hardin, Honore Dutrey and Bill Johnson waited. From the very first note, they knew. He played quietly behind Joe, softly in back of Joe, echoing after Joe. Someone yelled, "Let that youngster blow!" And Louis stepped forward and stood in front of Joe, and blew.

My boyhood dream had come true at last.

Louis stood in front of bands in Chicago, New York, California and Europe. On records, in Hollywood, on Broadway and on the radio. The little boy from New Orleans, Louisiana, from a part of town outside Storyville, in a corner called Back o' Town, in a section nicknamed The Battlefield, was just a lucky so and so.

I was so happy
I did not know what to do.
I had hit the big time.

LOUIS ARMSTRONG
AND HIS ORCH

Louis Armstrong
Author's Note

Louis Armstrong was born on August 4, 1901 to William "Willie" Armstrong and Mary Ann "Mayann" Albert. Shortly after his birth, his father left the family and Mayann sent Louis to live with his paternal grandmother, Josephine until he was five. A few years later William and MayAnn briefly reconciled and Mayann gave birth to Louis's sister Beatrice, nicknamed Mama Lucy.

Louis had many nicknames growing up— DipperMouth, Gatemouth, Rhythm Jaws, Iron Lips and Brass Lips, but his most famous nickname was Satchmo, the shortened version of Satchelmouth.

Louis' family struggled to survive on MayAnn's low wages, so he chipped in by picking up odd jobs and singing for pennies to help out his family. He entered the Fisk School for Boys at age seven but dropped out four years later to make money for his family. Louis became well known to the police for fighting, so when he shot a pistol into the air on New Year's Eve, he was arrested and sent before a judge. The judge sentenced him to an indefinite term at the Colored Waif's Home because he was considered a repeat offender.

Louis had many musical inspirations including Bill "Bojangles" Robinson, saxophonist Sydney Bechet, cornetists Bunk Johnson, Buddy Bolden and, of course, Joe Oliver.

When he left New Orleans in July of 1922 to play in Joe Oliver's band, he met his second wife, pianist Lil Hardin, who was also a member of King Oliver's Creole Band. Under Lil's influence, Louis eventually left Joe Oliver to play with bandleader Fletcher Henderson's band in another jazz town, Harlem, New York. In New York, Louis' career took off and he began recording with many of the popular singers of his day—Bessie Smith, Ma Rainey, Billie Holiday, Ella Fitzgerald and Clara Smith.

During one recording session where Louis was singing, he dropped the lyrics to the song "Heebie Jeebies." In order to not interrupt the session, he improvised by making up words and sounds to keep the recording session going. The end result was what we now call *scatting*, and the producers so loved Louis' made up version, they kept it on the recording. The end result forever altered what we now know as jazz singing.

Like many musicians, Louis travelled from town to town, band to band. That he could play his cornet at a pitch higher than a C, was a feat most cornetists and trumpeters could rarely achieve. He also played so loudly, he often had to stand twenty feet back from the rest of the band to not drown them out. His travels to Europe included performances for royalty.

When the bandleader Erskine Tate commented on his "stumpy" cornet, Louis tried out the trumpet and for the rest his career, it would be his instrument of choice. Despite his musical training at the Colored Waif's Home, Louis's embrouchure (the placement of the mouthpiece against his lip) was incorrect and resulted in his trademark scarred top lip. He suffered lip injuries throughout his career.

Best known for his hits *Hello Dolly*, *Ain't Misbehavin*, *Stardust*, *When the Saints Go Marchin In* and *What a Wonderful World*, he wrote over fifty songs. He was featured on over fifteen hundred sound recordings, thirty movies and several theater productions. Armstrong was the first black man to host a national radio show and the first jazz musician to write an autobiography.

Louis Armstrong and Duke Ellington made a famous jazz recording together in 1961 known as "The Great Summit." Included on that recording was a favorite version of Ellington and David Mack's upbeat song "Just a Lucky So and So," whose lyrics seemed to epitomize Armstrong's optimistic outlook.

Louis was honored with the Grammy Lifetime Achievement award and was inducted into the Rock and Roll Hall of Fame.

After performing for over fifty years, Louis Armstrong died of heart failure at the age of seventy in his Queens, New York home. He is still considered one of the greatest entertainers the world has ever seen.